This Notebook Belongs To:

_____

I0504060

_____

live MORE worry LESS

Time to head back to
Amazon to order
another book. If you
enjoyed this notebook,
we hope you will
share your opinion
by leaving a review
on Amazon.
Thank you,
Inspired Lines